Habit Stack

21 Small Life Changes to Improve Your Success, Wealth and Productivity

Published by **Restrolla Publishing**, www.restrolla.com

Copyright © 2017 by Philip Patterson.

ISBN-13: 978-1973748755
ISBN-10: 1973748754

Get Our Newest Books For FREE!

We love writing about ways to improve yourself.

If you want to receive a FREE COPY of any future books that we release, please sign up to our VIP list.

To show our appreciation, after confirming your subscription, you will be able to download the FREE BONUS report below.

www.restrolla.com/VIP-60EU7

Table of Contents

Introduction

Welcome to *Habit Stack.*

This book is packed with important information about habits. Before beginning, we talk about the concepts of habits and habit stacks. Do you realize they affect your life and the lives of your family and associates?

What do you know about hypnosis, self-hypnosis and meditation as modifiers of habits? My book tells you about these in as simple a way as possible. It does so in an inspiring way making you realize that by tapping into your subconscious you can do many things with your habits.

This book is written for the layperson, not for someone seeking a textbook. I believe that it is very informative and has many useful ideas for you to put into practice immediately.

There are six chapters, each chapter providing a stepping stone to the next. Each Chapter has a summary to refresh your memory about what's just been covered. This will help you to *consolidate what you learn*, chapter by chapter.

By the end, we will have covered *21 small changes and habits that will improve your success, productivity and happiness.*

Interested? Let's get started right away with Chapter 1...

Chapter 1: Habits and Stacking Habits

The word *habit* has a definition. A habit is a choice you **always** select and the subsequent action you **always** carry out. There has been research at Duke University that shows habits are responsible for about two-fifths of our behaviors on any particular day. Many habits are quite harmless, some are very good, while others need to be got rid of as soon as possible. Before we consider habits though we must first consider the *mind*.

The Mind

The mind is that part of a person that makes them aware of and allows them to use their environment and their experiences. It is the part of a person which enables them to feel and to think. There are two parts to the mind - the conscious mind and the subconscious mind.

The Conscious Mind

The conscious mind is the section of the mind that is used in everyday life and is only a small portion of our mind, about 10%. It is located in the prefrontal cortex, in what is called the frontal lobes, which are a part of the brain that is highly developed in humans. We use the conscious brain to think and to speak. The conscious mind generates sensations, thoughts and feelings.

Closely associated with the conscious mind is the preconscious mind. The preconscious holds memories frequently used but not normally in our thoughts. Examples of things held in the preconscious are our phone numbers, car license numbers, addresses, etc. The preconscious is between the conscious mind and the subconscious mind.

The Subconscious Mind

The subconscious mind is a fascinating part of the mind. There are few experts who doubt that it exists but no one really knows where it is. Part of it is in the limbic system of the brain and carries many important body functions such as the issuing of commands to keep the body's temperature at

98.6°F, to breathe, to keep the blood circulating, to execute each part of the sequence of steps in digesting food, etc.

The subconscious mind permanently stores everything that you have learned and experienced in your life. We can conveniently see the subconscious as a huge database of experience and information accumulated in your life. With hypnosis, all of this information can be unearthed. The subconscious mind ceaselessly tries to fit all things that you do, hence all of your habits, into a matrix that has been programmed into you, mainly when you were young.

Once again it is pointed out that the subconscious is a huge database of programs. If we are irritated then the *anger* program is loaded into our consciousness and what we do subsequently is consistent with this. Sometimes our actions may result in the programs for *shame* or *regret* to enter the conscious.

Habits are performed as a result of messages sent from the subconscious to the conscious, usually in response to a stimulus that the subconscious has been informed of by the senses. The rest of the habit is the program that has been loaded into the conscious and the subsequent actions.

Our lives are ruled by habits. Decisions result from whether we are angry, happy, bored, sad, or feeling frustrated and the habit we have as our reaction. Our hobbies and activities are often habits.

Habits often follow emotions. Emotions have three parts, a personal experience, a bodily response, and a behavioral response. Our habits are often this behavioral response. Emotions include anger, fear, surprise, happiness, sadness, embarrassment, excitement, shame, contempt, satisfaction, pride and amusement. Emotions are not very precise, but the habits they bring forth are.

Examples of emotions and the consequent habit in everyday life can easily be found. For our first example consider the anger you may feel if you are driving and someone passes you in the road. How do you deal with this? Do you have a stock response? If you do this is a habit.

For the second example consider the amusement you might feel if you see a fellow worker making derogatory jokes about some minority group. Again the habit may be how you deal with this. Your habits are often how you react to your emotions and they could be very important and will be discussed in great detail later.

Support Habits

Habits vary greatly in their size. The habit of *eating healthy food* involves a lot of time in learning what foods are healthy, preparing the food, consuming it etc. It is a huge habit and the smaller tasks, listed previously, are what are called *support* habits. Support habits are habits which support a larger habit.

Chapter Summary

- **A habit is a choice that is always made, followed by an action that is always carried out.**
- **The mind is that part of us which makes us aware and with which we think. The conscious mind is the part of the mind with which we feel and think.**
- **The subconscious mind is much bigger than the conscious mind and is a vast database of what we have learned, our experiences, programs that keep our bodies functioning and our habits.**
- **Large habits need support habits.**

Chapter 2: Stacking Habits Together

Having thoroughly considered the mind and existing habits, let us now have a look at how we might change our habits or acquire new ones. Some habits are good such as tidying up, exercising, walking the dog, driving properly... but some are not - such as leaving dishes unwashed, smoking, eating too much, losing one's temper.....

Before you start out in an examination of habits it is sensible to do something, which is extremely important.

Take an inventory of your life

- List the things that really matter to you.
- List your goals.

- Write down what you have accomplished. Be honest with yourself. Don't ignore things. You may need to ask others to help, as sometimes they can identify accomplishments you do not consider as such.
- List your regrets and again be honest.
- Now list your habits.

Large positive changes in life have been widely promoted by many people in many ways to happen quickly. However, it should be well known to everyone that there is hardly anyone who gets successful overnight. Moreover, most people will recognize the value of hard work and using many small habits in order to achieve their final goals. The key is to make a start with small things, repeating them until they become habits.

As an example, suppose your aim is to gain weight and become stronger. In order to do this, much more is required than just eating or training more. Using a Habit Stack, you begin with one thing. As a start, drink a protein smoothie with breakfast. This is done, each day, until it becomes a habit. Now proceed with something else such as how you train. Following this technique, you keep supplementing your life with new habits and routines and so build a stack, or stacks, of habits that will help you reach your goals of greater weight and strength.

In the book, Scott shows you how to do this in a step-by-step manner and how to build what he calls a habit stack of small habits. Scott presents all the information necessary to create these new useful habits.

This is done by what is called *synaptic pruning*. The connections between the *neurons* (basic building block of the nervous system) in your brain are called *synapses*. As years go by, your brain removes connections between neurons that are not used and develops connections between those, which are used often.

As an example, if you practice the guitar for a number of years, then the brain develops and strengthens connections between the neurons needed for guitar playing. The more frequently you play, the more powerful the connections become. In addition, these connections achieve greater speed and efficiency as you practice. This leads to expertise and what we will later call *flow*. A biological change has occurred leading to the development of skill.

However, for a person who has never played the guitar, there is no strengthening of these connections. Consequently, the brain removes unused connections and uses energy so freed to the building of connections needed for other reasons.

With this in mind, it is possible to explain the difference between brains of babies and adults. At birth, the brain is like a blank paper. There are a huge number of possibilities, but with no strong connections. Adults have discarded many of their neurons, however, there are strong connections between those they have in order to support their skills.

How does synaptic pruning assist in creating new habits? It turns out that synaptic pruning is involved with every habit you have. The brain supports your current behaviors with a strong network of neurons. The more something is repeated, the more powerful and effective the neuron connection involved becomes.

For example, your brain is probably very efficient at remembering to remove your pajamas each morning or to have your breakfast or to make your bed... or any of the myriad of habits you do each day. It is a wonderful fact that these strong connections can be used to start new habits.

> **The simplest method of inserting a new habit is to associate it with a current habit, i.e. you *stack the habits* on one another.**

This stacking of new habit 'on top' of existing habit is simpler to stack a new habit on top of an existing one than it is to create a completely new habit.

Examples of Stacking Habits

Here are some examples in no particular order of importance...

- *The Habit of Meditation:* After making my morning coffee, I will meditate for five minutes.
- *The Habit of Exercise:* After arising, I will do 20 deep knee bends.
- *The Habit of Cleaning Teeth In The Morning:* After breakfast, I brush my teeth.
- *The Habit of Counting Blessings:* Before I start dinner, I will remember one good thing from the day and write it down.
- *The Habit of Learning Something New:* When I get back from lunch break, I will learn one new thing in five minutes then record it then over another five minutes recall what I learned this time last week.
- *The Habit of Rinsing My Cup:* After I finish my coffee, I will rinse my cup.

Stacking works because your current habits have already been inserted in your brain. New habits are linked to an existing habit hence it is far easier to adhere to the new habit.

In order to begin, list your current daily habits, this includes everyday routines. Now, produce a second list of habits you'd like to start. Now, select one new habit and find the sensible existing habit of stacking it with.

Be sure that you stack complementary habits of sensible size. New habits at the start should be small. Later on, as they become ingrained they can be increased.

Chapter Summary

- **You should take an inventory of your life.**
- **Rapid changes toward major goals do NOT occur.**
- **New habits are easier to implement if stacked with existing habits.**
- **Start small when you begin stacking habits.**

Chapter 3: Habits Related to Health

Hierarchy of Needs

The psychologist Abraham Maslow, in 1943, published a widely accepted hierarchy of human needs. There were five levels of needs ranging from lowest (5) to highest (1). They were:

1. **Self-actualization needs**

Such things as sport, art, knowledge.....

2. **Esteem needs**

Prestige, Feelings of accomplishment

3. **Belongingness and Love needs**

Intimate relationships, friends

4. **Safety needs**

Security, safety

5. **Physiological needs**

Food, water, warmth, rest

All of our habits can be placed into one or other of these need categories. Those involving health, which we look at this chapter are among those ranked 5 in the hierarchy.

Inventory of your life

It was suggested that you carry out an inventory of your life in which the last instruction was to make a list of your habits. If you do not have the following habit on your list then place it there. It is extremely important and will provide a means to structure your other habits.

Habit 1: Make a daily checklist of tasks to be done

Most people who are successful have one. Presidents, Prime Ministers, CEOs and other leaders often have subordinates prepare them. The reason for this is to remove the guesswork about what should be done. The wise staff knows the needs and habits of their employers and include such things as dining, gym sessions and social meetings in with the work commitments. If possible they also leave spaces for the leaders to insert personal items.

By setting up these checklists important things that have to be done are scheduled and must be carried out. If you are preparing this checklist make sure that you have some means by which you can assign a rank of importance to the tasks so that you ensure that the really important tasks are carried out. Here are some benefits of checklists.

- They remove decision-making about what to do.
- They ensure things are done.
- Time is saved and time is precious.

What Habits Should You Have For Good Health?

The list below is probably not exhaustive but includes many things you need to consider. Some of these such as diet, exercise, and meditation are huge habits and probably need many support habits.

1. **Eat a good diet**. This was mentioned in the previous chapter and is a very large habit requiring many support habits.
2. **Exercise regularly**. Every authority on health puts great value on exercise. It should never be neglected.

3. **Get enough sleep.** Even if you have a good diet and regular exercise but get less than seven hours sleep frequently you are in danger of great harm. A shortage of sleep in the short-term causes such things as lack of alertness, bad temper, being accident-prone, having difficulty in concentrating. In the long-term, a lack of sleep can be very serious with consequences such as loss of libido and high blood pressure.

4. **Avoid stress.** Stress is something that must be controlled. Stress is the result of what is seen as threat and the body's reaction to it. Everybody sometimes has what is referred to as acute stress when a dangerous situation arises. Such stress is short-lived and good. However, there is something called chronic stress that goes on and on and can be the cause of serious health problems. There are many possible causes for this: a failing relationship, an unpleasant job you have to do, a sick family member are among obvious causes. There are ways of combatting stress such as meditation and yoga. The topic of stress is worth a book on its own.

5. **Stop smoking.** All medical authorities are against smoking. The evidence against it is overwhelming. If you are a smoker then stop as soon as you can.

6. **Avoid too much sun.** Sunshine is beneficial for us in the short-term but not to excess. Most facial wrinkling

and some types of cancer are the results of too much sun.

7. **Sex is an important part of most people's lives.** Communication is vital for a satisfying sex life.
8. **Everyone needs some fresh air**. This has to be factored into a healthy lifestyle.
9. **It is sensible to have medical checkups regularly** and to be tested for medical conditions that may occur in your family.
10. **Learn to meditate.** This is possibly new to most readers and is discussed at length below.

Meditation is often associated with the Eastern religions, where meditation techniques have been used for many centuries. In the past fifty years, there has been a great increase in the use of the techniques of meditation among Western peoples, particularly for relaxation and mindfulness.

Successful meditating goes hand in hand with successful concentration, and the factors, which help concentration, are the relaxation of the body, a quiet and peaceful environment, and emotional peace. Meditation needs to become a habit.

The purpose of this meditation is to reach a more relaxed state to increase the ability to concentrate, to raise mental and physical awareness, and to attain a higher level of thinking activity and consciousness.

Chapter Summary

- **Habit 1 is, 'Every day you must have a checklist.'**
- **Good Health Requires Many Habits, Some Of Which Are Listed Below.**
- **Eat A Good Diet**
- **Exercise**
- **Get Enough Sleep**
- **Minimize Stress**
- **Practice No Smoking**
- **See To A Need For Fresh Air**
- **Get Regular Medical Checkups**
- **Practice Meditation**

Chapter 4: Habits Related to Success

Control

Control is the ability to have influence on or to direct the behavior of people or events. The ability of a teacher to control his or her classes is a good example. The capability of that teacher is severely handicapped when there are deficiencies in that ability even if they are very knowledgeable in what they teach. Another example is provided by the driver of a truck. If they do not have the habit of being able to control the truck properly and it veers all over the place then he or she becomes a danger on the road. The control of habits is quite important and for the successful control of some habits, it is vital to exercise good self-control.

Self-Control

Self-control is the ability to control oneself, particularly one's wants and emotions, often expressed as habits. Rather than surrender to immediate impulses, a bad habit, we must learn to consider different options, and avoid actions that could be a cause for regret.

Another name for self-control is willpower. By using it we can be focused; it is vital for most significant achievement. It is believed by some scientists that we only possess a limited supply of willpower. Self-control uses a lot of mental energy and a lot of glucose, the main fuel of the brain, is consumed. The result is called *ego depletion*.

Ego depletion describes a situation where self- control is absent. When a person is stressed he or she is more likely to yield to temptation than when more relaxed. Whether self-control is finite is a source of active research.

There are examples of prisoners of war who have kept up their self-control throughout their imprisonment. Senator John McCain, who ran for US President in 2008, is a good example. He was cruelly treated for more than 5 years as a prisoner in Vietnam however he always maintained his self-control. The amount of self-control in some people is very great. Such people will find the discarding of bad habits and the stacking of new positive habits quite straightforward.

Self-control is such an important quality that practicing it becomes a **habit.**

Flow

It was mentioned before that when involved in activities a person has practiced thoroughly they often get a very positive feeling called *flow*. Due to their practice, the activity has turned into a habit and it is or is almost fun. If in flow then you seem to enter another state.

When you are in flow, you pay great attention to whatever it is that you are doing. You do not need to concentrate, as the concentration appears automatic. Here is how a great gymnast described flow, "The performance is a struggle, but the focus is like breathing. You don't even think about it." A professional dancer said," You are totally involved in your actions. The moves are a habit. You're completely absorbed in your dancing. It is almost dreamlike. Time passes very quickly".

Great self-control is always demonstrated by outstanding athletes. It is extraordinary how they focus and get flow, seemingly without effort and under the extraordinary pressures of competition, with thousands watching their every move. It is the habits, supporting their habit of self-control, which makes this possible.

What are these habits?

1. You must be able to concentrate attention on the activity. Doing this enables you to achieve flow by joining your consciousness with the activity. No matter what worthwhile activity the flow will come if doing this becomes a habit.
2. Acquire the habit of forgetting time during your activity. If you want to flow then you must concentrate on the activity, so you can adjust to possibly changing circumstances.
3. Put away thoughts of the past or the future. If you allow yourself time to think or worry about the past or future then those thoughts will interfere with what is happening. Don't do anything to take you out of the moment. Flow is in the present tense.
4. Be both relaxed and alert. Put aside concerns except for concerns specific to what you're doing.
5. Flow does not just happen. You must train for flow. A discipline that makes you focus on the present will enhance your ability to flow. There are many activities that do this. Among them most types of serious

dancing, most types of weightlifting and Oriental martial arts. All require awareness and movement to focus attention. All techniques of hypnosis and meditation instill the ability to concentrate on whatever is happening at the moment, no matter what it may be.

Flow is a characteristic of people with great self-control. They get this flow by accessing their subconscious mind.

In this book, we emphasize the benefits of stacking habits. It was mentioned that new habits are most effectively acquired when they are tacked onto existing habits. You may well ask "What will I stack the habits above with?

These habits, all related to self-control, could be conveniently stacked with your possibly new habit of self-control. In the next chapter, we will show a concrete example of the five habits above in a work situation.

We have talked about meditation as it offers a way for anyone to access his or her subconscious. Realize that if we lack an ability to dip into its extraordinary potential self-control will be very hard to achieve.

As well as meditation the techniques of hypnosis and self-hypnosis offer some methods by which we can access the subconscious. These techniques are briefly described below. If you believe that one or more could help you then they could become new habit stacks. By describing self-hypnosis in detail, we will demonstrate this.

Hypnosis

Hypnosis can be described as a conscious state where people enter a trance and seem to be without the ability to carry out voluntary action. They cooperate, as much as possible, with the suggestions of the person who induced the trance. If someone is being hypnotized he or she is not put into a deep sleep, and it is not possible for him or her to be coerced to do something they know to be wrong such killing someone. A person who is undergoing hypnosis is aware of their environment and situation.

Hypnosis is used in a treatment called hypnotherapy, which usually attempts to bring to light suppressed memories or the modification of behavior. It is useful if someone is undergoing hypnotherapy, to learn the techniques of self-hypnosis, which can be carried out at home, so as to assist the sessions with the hypnotherapist.

Here is quite a full description of self-hypnosis to illustrate how it could become a habit stack.

Self-Hypnosis

Self-hypnosis is self-induced hypnosis and is sometimes known as autohypnosis.

It is possible to use self-hypnosis to modify emotions, attitudes, and habits. Self-hypnosis can be used in sport to improve performance. Pain or from stress related problems can be helped by self-hypnosis. The advice of a doctor or qualified person is advised if you are already in any sort of professional therapy.

Here is an effective sequence of support habits for the habit *practice self-hypnosis.*

1. Find a quiet place
2. Sit or lie in a comfortable position and uncross your feet and legs.
3. Inhale deeply and inform yourself that your eyes are getting tired, that you desire to fall into sleep. This should be repeated for it to work. If you don't fall asleep then don't worry but keep repeating it quietly.

4. Feel your body relax and become limp then count back mentally from 5 to 0. Tell yourself as you count that you're becoming ever more relaxed.

5. Remain like this for a few minutes, all the time your focus should be on breathing.

6. Notice how your chest and diaphragm rises and falls.

7. Observe that your body has become relaxed even though you are not trying to relax it.

8. The less you try to relax the greater the relaxation.

At this stage after these eight support habits, you have reached self-hypnosis.

Once in a self-hypnotic condition you are able to make, what is called post-hypnotic suggestions to assist you in whatever you desire.

Here is how you should make these suggestions.

1. Say exactly what you mean.

2. Be reassuring, positive, and confident.

3. Refer to the present time.

4. Be realistic. If you desire to improve your performance in swimming it would not be realistic to give yourself the suggestion," I will soon be world champion," unless you are world class.

5. Repeating suggestions is of great importance. If you only repeat a suggestion once then it will be ineffectual.

6. Visualization of what you want during your self-hypnotic suggestions is very useful. Try and have a clear mental picture of your desired.

When ready, come back to the room you are in by counting up from 1 to 5. Tell yourself that you are becoming aware of your surroundings and at the count of five open your eyes.

Chapter Summary

- **Acquire the habit of self-control.**
- **Practice good habits that support self-control until you get flow in the activities you pursue which need improvement.**
- **Meditation, Hypnosis, and Self-Hypnosis are means by which the sub-conscious mind can be reprogrammed to enhance self-control.**

Chapter 5: Habits Related to Wealth and Productivity

The following headings are habits that are very important in any quest for wealth and increased productivity.

Use your daily Checklist

The first habit you were told to perform in this book was to make a daily checklist of tasks that have been prioritized. This habit is crucially important and if you really want to succeed cannot be stressed enough. If you do not make a daily checklist then it becomes much harder to acquire the habit of practicing self-control.

Don't Waste Time

- This is a no brainer.
- Time is like land; there is only a limited supply of it.

- Time is irreplaceable and once it has gone then it is gone forever.
- Much of the demands on our time are rubbish.
- Many hours are spent every year in the doing of things that we would probably be better not doing.
- What is an hour of your time really worth?
- We are here to achieve and not just to do.
- Make sure that you do the right thing and not just absorb yourself in doing things right.
- Don't hesitate in abandoning habits and rituals such as checking social media.

Pay Off Debt

This needs to be a habit and NOT an optional extra.

- Sadly when some people get into debt they take on more debt in order to pay off the previous debt and as they do so they fall deeper into debt. They reduce their credit score.
- If you pay off your debt then it is a much better option than investing as you do not pay any taxes on debts that you pay off whereas you usually have to pay taxes on interest that you get from investments
- If you pay off debts then you reduce stress.

- Once an asset is paid off then any increase in value becomes yours and this is particularly so in the case of real estate.
- If you do not pay off your debts then you have to deal with people who lend money and these are often very unpleasant people. They are in the business of making money and not making friends.

Count the Cost

Many people fail to do this and end up paying a lot in the long run. They are often the sorts of people who wonder where the money goes. If you are one of them then you need to acquire the habit of counting the cost. This also applies to someone in business. Business costs must be tracked otherwise serious damage can be done to your enterprise.

Here is a very simple example. Supermarkets often put confectionery near the checkout. The harassed shopper sees a delicious Hershey bar for a $1 and decides to buy it. They go shopping at the supermarket three days a week. They buy three bars each week. There are fifty-two weeks in a year. They are on holiday for two weeks so they buy the three bars fifty times. **Over a year that is $150!! Ouch!**

Be Positive

If at work you are an unhappy or angry person you will lower the outlook and morale of many of your colleagues. You may even threaten their health, particularly if you are the boss. Everyone wants to collaborate with happy, optimistic, positive and cheerful people; few wish to be around or have to endure those who are angry, sullen or moody.

Learn a new skill

Sometimes this is vital and, if you don't, your very job may disappear. This is happening with ever-greater frequency. Many are the young person who was told in the 1970s that learning to use a typewriter was a passport to job security. This advice was not accurate. Modern offices seem to be bereft of typewriters. Indeed the only place you can be sure of finding one now is in a museum!

The learning of new skills will make you more useful and employable. Be careful in learning new skills that you do so in a way, which helps your goals.
Suppose you were keen to learn a new computer language called *Kax*. Let's use the support habits listed in Chapter 4.

1. You must be able to concentrate attention on Kax.

2. As far as possible forget time while learning Kax. It is what you put into the time you're learning in not the time itself that is important.

3. Dispense with thoughts of the past without Kax or the future with it.

4. Study Kax when you are both relaxed and alert. When you do so put aside concerns that are not related to the task of learning Kax.

You can see the application of the supporting habits for the learning of Kax.

The learning of new skills is particularly important if you embrace the next habit.

Apply for new jobs

This is not a good habit to have if you are completely happy with your current position. However, sometimes the current position has become impossible and you must move on. In such a case you should acquire a habit stack of applying for new jobs.

Never invest more than you can afford to lose

This should be well known, however, it is best illustrated with an example. Few have not heard of Bitcoin and other cryptocurrencies. Should you buy cryptocurrency as soon as you can? Some experts say so, with some believing that its value will keep rising, with one Bitcoin valued at $100,000 inside a decade. Cryptocurrencies may appear odd now, but it is sensible to recall that when Apple, Microsoft, and other technology companies began moving forward during the 1980s, there were people who thought personal computers had no future. History has proved these people were wrong and people who were astute enough to buy shares in Apple or Microsoft are financially very happy now.

Despite this, you must always exercise care and caution, the rise in the price of an asset does not mean that its true worth is increasing. There are many good examples of this throughout the history of investment, with a very unfortunate one being the U.S. real estate boom of the late 2000s. Sometimes prices are driven up by hype and outright lies. It is always sensible to remember that if something ascends it usually descends.

Spread your investments

Within any investment portfolio you have, you should have different investments, there are many to select from. This process goes by the name of, 'spreading the risk', do not forget the saying that *you should not put all your eggs in only one basket.*

Chapter Summary

- Acquire these habits.
- Use your daily checklist.
- Don't waste time.
- Pay off debt.
- Count the cost.
- Be positive
- Learn a new skill.
- Possibly apply for a new job.
- Never invest more than you can afford to lose.
- Spread your assets.

Chapter 6: Miscellaneous Habits

This is the final chapter in this book and I will consider some habits, which can make real and positive changes. Then I will finish with 21 habits we have considered thoroughly.

Take an interest in the world

This is similar to the habit I urged you to embrace in the last chapter of learning new skills. This is a broader interpretation of the same mindset which enables you to get a grasp of what is really happening and preventing you from becoming a backward looking irrelevance.

Look after your children

Having children is one of the greatest privileges we are given. We are only stewards of our children and s parents our duty is to prepare them for a life in a world which we will only see some of. There was a brilliant song sung by Harry Chapin that went, "My child arrived just the other day....But there were planes to catch, and bills to pay...He learned to walk while I was away."

If your child says they want to do something with you then make a habit of finding the time to do so. They are only young for a short time. Soon they won't want to know you unless you've found the time to be with them while they're young.

Confide but wisely

Discuss with those who are close to you how you feel. You must exercise great here. There are few things more frustrating to your friends, colleagues or members of your family than someone who keeps on loading them with their problems. Their companionship and advice is wonderful but do not abuse them.

Never forget the story of the child who cried, "Wolf," all the time. Frequently he said he was being threatened by a vicious wolf. Initially, his friends and relatives were concerned however he made false claims so often they ignored him. Sadly the day came when the wolf was real. However, nobody responded to his cries for help and the wolf had a great lunch!

Learn to deal with your emotions

In dealing with negative emotion, we have to be determined. Emotions can be very painful and it is generally recognized that ignoring an emotion is not a valid procedure. It is possible in the short-term, sometimes even longer, however eventually, you will have to come to grips with the emotion. Strategies for this are set out below.

- Pinpoint the root of the emotion. What does this actually mean? Usually, it is not the cause of the emotion. Often the cause is obvious, however, your subsequent reaction to that cause could be more of a problem. Clearly, there are few not affected by the sudden death of someone close but sometimes this seems to trigger a most unfortunate reaction. You must identify the reason for your behavior. This may be preventing you from moving on. Could something from the past that your subconscious has buried be the cause of this?
- You must learn to handle how you have thought and acted then move on.
- Discuss your emotions with people you trust who are prepared to listen to you but don't overdo this as we pointed out in the previous chapter.

- Concern yourself in the present and don't worry about possibilities, which are not likely in future. It is so easy to waste time in worry about things that won't happen.
- Be critical about the way you cope, in your life, with negative emotions. If you use alcohol, smoking, comfort food, and drugs as strategies then you need to forsake them as soon as you can.
- Realize that on occasion a negative emotion develops into a support or crutch. Don't let worry, fear, anger and any other emotion that is negative hold you back. You have to learn when they are
- Mindfulness, self-hypnosis, and meditation are very useful in coping with your emotions.
- It is so important to be grateful. You may think things are hard for you but always you will find they are much harder for someone else who has succeeded despite their problems. Consider the inspiring story of Brian Acton. In 2009 Brian Acton was a software engineer who had had 12 years experience at Yahoo and Apple. He wanted promotion and applied, and without success, for jobs at Twitter and at Facebook. Not letting these rejections discourage him he teamed up with another man called Jan Koum and developed the app called WhatsApp. Facebook ended up purchasing this app for $19 billion!

Develop Your Spirituality

Spirituality can defined as connection to something that is greater than any of us. It is not necessarily connected to a particular religion, although devout adherents of most religions can find within their faiths the answers to all their questions about such matters. The development of one's spirituality is a habit, which once started must never be neglected. In some ways, this habit can be seen as the logical developments of earlier suggested habits, which were *to learn a new skill* and *to take an interest in the world*. Spirituality can be seen as a habit stack with the earlier habits as supporting habits.

Chapter Summary

- **Take an interest in the world**
- **Do not neglect your children**
- **Confide but wisely**
- **Learn to deal with your emotions**
- **Develop your spirituality**

Perspective

Mastery of your habits is one of the foundations of success. If you wish to master life's challenges you have to master your habits. This book has thoroughly covered why this is so important and 21 Important Habits that you've learned are listed below.

21 Small Changes and Habits to Live By

- **Make a daily checklist**
- **Eat a good diet**
- **Exercise regularly**
- **Get enough sleep**
- **Avoid stress**
- **Communicate with your loved ones**
- **Practice meditation**
- **Practice self-control**

- **Practice your calling until you achieve flow.**
- **Practice self-hypnosis**
- **Don't waste time**
- **Pay off debt**
- **Count the cost of repeated small actions over time**
- **Be positive**
- **Learn new skills**
- **Never invest more than you can afford to lose**
- **Take an interest in the world**
- **Do not neglect your children**
- **Confide but wisely**
- **Learn to deal with your emotions**
- **Develop your spirituality**

My book has therefore shown some of the great things that can be done if you learn to control your habits rather than just do them. It has demonstrated the great importance of this. It should have helped you make the decision to practice self-hypnotism and meditation as some of the means by which you can do this.

If you do, you are far more likely to be a winner.

Good luck with your quest for success. You deserve it!

And finally... If you liked the book, I would like to ask you to do me the favor of leaving a review on Amazon.

Please go to your account on Amazon, or paste in the link below into your browser.

http://amzn.to/2vz8qCM

Thank you very much!

www.ingramcontent.com/pod-product-compliance
Lightning Source LLC
Chambersburg PA
CBHW071241220526
45468CB00002B/950